Violin

John Kember and Roger Smith

Violin Sight-Reading 1

Déchiffrage pour le violon 1
Vom-Blatt-Spiel auf der Geige 1

A fresh approach / Nouvelle approche
Eine erfrischend neue Methode

ED 12836
ISMN M-2201-2383-2

Mainz · London · Madrid · New York · Paris · Prague · Tokyo · Toronto

ED 12836

British Library Cataloguing-in-Publication Data.
A catalogue record for this book is available from the British Library
ISMN M-2201-2383-2

French translation: Agnès Ausseur
German translation: Ute Corleis
Design by adamhaystudio.com
Music setting and page layout by Jackie Leigh
Printed in Germany S&Co.8042

Contents
Sommaire/Inhalt

Preface

Violin Sight-Reading 1 aims to establish good practice and provide an early introduction to the essential skill of sight-reading.

Sight-reading given as 'homework' is of little value unless the result is heard by the teacher. Ideally, sight-reading in some form should become a regular part of a student's routine each time they get out the violin.

This book aims to establish the habit early in a student's violin playing. Of course, names of notes and time values need to be thoroughly known and understood, but equally sight-reading is helped by an awareness of shape and direction.

There are eight sections in this book, each of which gradually introduces new notes, rhythms, articulations, dynamics and Italian terms in a logical sequence, much as you would find in a beginner's violin tutor. The emphasis is on providing idiomatic tunes and structures as well as sight-reading exercises designed to give the player confidence.

Each section begins with several solo examples and concludes with duets and accompanied pieces, enabling the player to gain experience of sight-reading within the context of ensemble playing.

Section 1 uses open strings, first plucked then bowed, together with simple rhythms in 4/4 time.

Section 2 begins with open strings in 2-, 3- and 4-time before introducing the 1st finger.

Section 3 adds the 2nd finger, together with the key signatures of G, D and A major.

Section 4 adds the 3rd finger and the key of E major. The use of quavers (eighth notes) is introduced in simple time.

Section 5 introduces the keys of C, F and B♭ major.

Section 6 uses all keys so far introduced and adds both dotted rhythms and slurs.

Section 7 introduces counting in quaver beats (eighth notes) in 3/8 time and brings in 'open string shifts' in the solo section. Semiquavers are introduced.

Section 8 concludes book 1 and is devoted to compound time, both 6/8 and 9/8.

To the pupil: why sight-reading?

When you are faced with a new piece and asked to play it, whether at home, in a lesson, or in an exam or audition, there is no one there to help you – except yourself! Sight-reading tests your ability to read the time and notes correctly, and to observe the phrasing and dynamics quickly.

The aim of this book is to help you to teach yourself. The book gives guidance on what to look for and how best to prepare in a very short time by observing the time and key signatures, the shape of the melody, and the marks of expression. These short pieces progress gradually to help you build up your confidence and observation, and enable you to sight-read accurately. At the end of each section, there are duets to play with your teacher or friends, and pieces with piano accompaniment which will test your ability to sight-read while something else is going on. This is a necessary skill when playing with a band, orchestra or other ensemble.

If you sight-read something every time you play your violin you will be amazed how much better you will become. Remember, if you can sight-read most of the tunes you are asked to learn you will be able to concentrate on the 'tricky bits' and complete them quickly.

Think of the tunes in this book as mini-pieces and try to learn them quickly and correctly, then when you are faced with real sight-reading you will be well equipped to succeed on a first attempt.

You are on your own now!

Préface

Le propos de ce recueil de déchiffrage pour le violon est de fournir une première initiation et un entraînement solide aux principes de la lecture à vue.

Le déchiffrage imposé comme un « travail » ne présente pas grand intérêt s'il n'est supervisé par le maître. L'idéal serait que le déchiffrage prenne régulièrement place dans la routine de travail de l'élève à chaque fois qu'il prend son violon.

L'objectif est ici d'établir l'habitude de la lecture à vue très tôt dans l'étude du violon. Le déchiffrage suppose, bien sûr, que les noms et les valeurs de notes soient complètement assimilés et compris mais il s'appuie également sur la reconnaissance des contours et de la direction.

Ce volume comporte huit sections correspondant à l'introduction graduelle de notes, de rythmes, de phrasés, de nuances et de termes italiens nouveaux selon la progression logique rencontrée dans une méthode de violon pour débutant. La démarche consiste à fournir des airs et des structures idiomatiques propres au violon ainsi que des exercices de déchiffrage conçus en vue de développer l'assurance de l'interprète.

Chaque section débute par plusieurs exemples de solos et se termine par des duos et des pièces accompagnées afin de familiariser le violoniste avec l'expérience de la lecture à vue dans le cadre d'une exécution collective.

La section 1 recourt aux cordes à vide, tout d'abord pincées puis jouées avec l'archet, et aux rythmes simples dans une mesure à 4/4.

La section 2 débute par les cordes à vide et des mesures à 2, 3 et 4 temps avant d'introduire le premier doigt.

La section 3 ajoute le deuxième doigt et les armures des tonalités de *sol* majeur, *ré* majeur et *la* majeur.

La section 4 ajoute le troisième doigt et la tonalité de *mi* mineur. Les croches y apparaissent dans des mesures simples.

La section 5 introduit les tonalités de *do* majeur, *fa* majeur et *si*♭ majeur.

La section 6 reprend toutes les tonalités vues jusqu'à ce point et ajoute les rythmes pointés et les liaisons de phrasé.

La section 7 introduit la battue d'une croche par temps dans la mesure à 3/8 et les « déplacements sur cordes à vide » dans la section en solo, ainsi que quelques doubles croches.

La section 8 qui conclut le volume 1, se concentre sur les mesures composées à 6/8 et à 9/8.

A l'élève : Pourquoi le déchiffrage ?

Lorsque vous vous trouvez face à un nouveau morceau que l'on vous demande de jouer, que ce soit chez vous, pendant une leçon ou lors d'un examen ou d'une audition, personne d'autre ne peut vous aider que vous-même ! Le déchiffrage met à l'épreuve votre capacité à lire correctement les rythmes et les notes et à observer rapidement le phrasé et les nuances.

Ce recueil se propose de vous aider à vous entraîner vous-même. Il vous oriente sur ce que vous devez repérer et sur la meilleure manière de vous préparer en un laps de temps très court en sachant observer les indications de mesure et l'armure de la clef, les contours de la mélodie et les indications expressives. Ces pièces brèves, en progressant par étapes, vous feront prendre de l'assurance, aiguiseront vos observations et vous permettront de lire à vue avec exactitude et aisance. A la fin de chaque section figurent des duos que vous pourrez jouer avec votre professeur ou des amis et des morceaux avec accompagnement de piano qui mettront à l'épreuve votre capacité de déchiffrage pendant que se déroule une autre partie. Celle-ci est indispensable pour jouer dans un groupe, un orchestre ou un ensemble.

Vous serez surpris de vos progrès si vous déchiffrez une pièce à chaque fois que vous vous mettez au violon. N'oubliez pas que si vous êtes capable de lire à vue la plupart des morceaux que vous allez étudier, vous pourrez vous concentrer sur les passages difficiles et les assimiler plus vite.

Considérez ces pages comme des « mini-morceaux » et essayez de les apprendre rapidement et sans erreur de manière à ce que, devant un véritable déchiffrage, vous soyez bien armé pour réussir dès la première lecture.

Vous êtes désormais seul !

Vorwort

Vom-Blatt-Spiel auf der Geige 1 möchte zu einer guten Übetechnik verhelfen und frühzeitig für die Einführung der grundlegenden Fähigkeit des Blatt-Spiels sorgen.

Vom-Blatt-Spiel als ‚Hausaufgabe' aufzugeben hat wenig Sinn, wenn das Ergebnis nicht vom Lehrer überprüft wird. Idealerweise sollte das Vom-Blatt-Spiel in irgendeiner Form ein regelmäßiger Bestandteil des Übens werden.

Dieses Buch hat zum Ziel, bereits von Anfang an diese Gewohnheit im Geigenspiel des Schülers zu verankern. Natürlich muss man die Notennamen und Notenwerte komplett kennen und verstanden haben, aber genauso wird das Vom-Blatt-Spiel durch das Bewusstsein für Form und Richtung unterstützt.

Das Buch hat acht Teile, die nach und nach neue Noten, Rhythmen, Artikulation, Dynamik und italienische Begriffe in einer logischen Abfolge einführen - ganz ähnlich, wie man es in einer Geigenschule für Anfänger auch finden würde. Der Schwerpunkt liegt sowohl auf dem Bereitstellen passender Melodien und Strukturen als auch auf Blatt-Spiel Übungen, die darauf ausgerichtet sind, dem Spieler Selbstvertrauen zu geben.

Jeder Teil beginnt mit einigen Solobeispielen und endet mit Duetten und begleiteten Stücken, damit man auch beim Zusammenspiel mit anderen Erfahrungen mit dem Blattspiel sammeln kann.

Teil 1 verwendet nur leere Saiten, erst gezupft, dann gestrichen, zusammen mit einfachen Rhythmen im 4/4-Takt.

Teil 2 beginnt mit leeren Saiten im 2/4-, 3/4- und 4/4-Takt, bevor der erste Finger hinzugenommen wird.

Teil 3 fügt den zweiten Finger hinzu, zusammen mit den Vorzeichen für G-, D- und A-Dur.

Teil 4 verwendet den dritten Finger und die Tonart E-Dur. Der Gebrauch von Achtelnoten in einfachen Taktarten wird eingeführt.

Teil 5 führt die Tonarten C- , F- und B-Dur ein.

Teil 6 benutzt alle Vorzeichen, die bisher eingeführt wurden. Neu hinzu kommen punktierte Rhythmen und Bindungen.

Teil 7 will das Zählen von Achtelschlägen im 3/8-Takt näherbringen und bezieht im Soloteil Lagenwechsel mit ein. Außerdem kommen Sechzehntelnoten hinzu.

Teil 8 beschließt Band 1 und widmet sich den zusammengesetzten Taktarten – sowohl 6/8 als auch 9/8.

An den Schüler: Warum Vom-Blatt-Spiel?

Wenn du dich einem neuen Musikstück gegenüber siehst und gebeten wirst, es zu spielen, egal, ob zu Hause, im Unterricht, in einem Examen oder einem Vorspiel, gibt es niemanden, der dir helfen kann – nur du selbst! Das Blatt-Spiel testet die Fähigkeit, die Taktart und die Noten richtig zu lesen sowie Phrasierungen und Dynamik schnell zu erfassen.

Ziel dieses Buches ist es, dir beim Selbstunterricht behilflich zu sein. Das Buch zeigt dir, worauf du achten sollst und wie du dich in sehr kurzer Zeit am besten vorbereitest. Das tust du, indem du dir Takt- und Tonart sowie den Verlauf der Melodie und die Ausdruckszeichen genau anschaust. Die kurzen Musikstücke steigern sich allmählich, um zum einen dein Vertrauen und deine Beobachtungsgabe aufzubauen, zum anderen auch, um dich dazu zu befähigen, exakt vom Blatt zu spielen. Am Ende jeden Teils stehen Duette, die du mit deinem Lehrer oder deinen Freunden spielen kannst. Außerdem gibt es Stücke mit Klavierbegleitung, die deine Fähigkeit im Blatt-Spiel überprüfen, während gleichzeitig etwas anderes abläuft. Das ist eine wesentliche Fähigkeit, wenn man mit einer Band, einem Orchester oder einer anderen Musikgruppe zusammenspielt.

Wenn du jedes Mal, wenn du Geige spielst, auch etwas vom Blatt spielst, wirst du überrascht sein, wie sehr du dich verbesserst. Denke daran: wenn du die meisten Melodien, die du spielen sollst, vom Blatt spielen kannst, kannst du dich auf die ‚schwierigen Teile' konzentrieren und diese viel schneller beherrschen.

Stelle dir die Melodien in diesem Buch als ‚Ministücke' vor und versuche, sie schnell und korrekt zu lernen. Wenn du dann wirklich vom Blatt spielen musst, wirst du bestens ausgerüstet sein, um gleich beim ersten Versuch erfolgreich zu sein.

Jetzt bist du auf dich selbst gestellt!

Section 1 – Open strings
Section 1 – Cordes à vide
Teil 1 – Leere Saiten

Three steps to success

1. **Look at the top number of the time signature (4)**. It shows the number of beats in a bar. Tap (clap, sing or play on one note) the rhythm, feeling the pulse throughout. Count at least one bar of the time signature in your head to set up the pulse before you tap or play.

2. **Look for patterns**. While tapping the rhythm, look at the melodic shape and notice movement by step, skips, repeated notes and sequences (a short repeated melodic phrase which often rises or falls by step).

3. **Keep going**. Remember, a wrong note or rhythm can be corrected the next time you play it. If you stop, you have doubled the mistake!

Trois étapes vers la réussite

1. **Observez le chiffre supérieur de l'indication de mesure (4)**. Il indique le nombre de pulsations contenues par mesure. Frappez (dans les mains, chantez ou jouez sur une seule note) le rythme tout en maintenant une pulsation intérieure constante. Comptez mentalement au moins une mesure complète pour installer la pulsation avant de frapper ou de jouer chaque pièce.

2. **Repérez les motifs**. Tout en frappant le rythme, observez les contours de la mélodie et relevez les mouvements par degrés, les sauts d'intervalles, les notes répétées et les séquences (courtes phrases mélodiques répétées progressant généralement par degrés ascendants ou descendants).

3. **Ne vous arrêtez pas**. N'oubliez pas que vous pourrez corriger une fausse note ou un rythme inexact la prochaine fois que vous jouerez. En vous interrompant, vous doublez la faute !

Drei Schritte zum Erfolg

1. **Schaue dir die obere Zahl der Taktangabe an (4)**. Diese zeigt die Anzahl der Schläge in einem Takt an. Schlage (klatsche, singe oder spiele auf einer Note) den Rhythmus, wobei du immer das Metrum spürst. Zähle mindestens einen Takt lang die Taktangabe im Kopf, um das Metrum zu verinnerlichen, bevor du klopfst oder spielst.

2. **Achte auf Muster**. Schaue dir die melodische Form an, während du den Rhythmus schlägst und achte auf Bewegungen in Schritten oder Sprüngen, sich wiederholende Noten und Sequenzen (eine kurze, sich wiederholende melodische Phrase, die oft schrittweise ansteigt oder abfällt).

3. **Spiele immer weiter**. Denke daran: eine falsche Note oder ein falscher Rhythmus kann beim nächsten Mal korrigiert werden. Wenn du aber aufhörst zu spielen, verdoppelst du den Fehler!

Section 1 – Open strings
Section 1 – Cordes à vide
Teil 1 – Leere Saiten

Open strings.   Cordes à vide.   Leere Saiten.

1.

2.

3.

4.

Open strings – mixed.   Cordes à vide mélangées.   Verschiedene leere Saiten.

5.

6.

Open strings – change of rhythm.   Cordes à vide – changement de rythme.   Leere Saiten – Rhythmuswechsel.

15.

16.

17.

18.

Note against note.

Note contre note.

Erstes Zusammenspiel.

19.

Pupil / Elève / Schüler

Teacher / Professeur / Lehrer

20.

21.

Independent rhythms.   Rythmes indépendants.   Erweitertes Zusammenspiel.

22.

23.

24.

25.

26.

27.

Section 2 – Open strings in 2-, 3- and 4-time
Section 2 – Cordes à vide dans des mesures à 2, 3 et 4 temps
Teil 2 – Leere Saiten im 2/4-, 3/4- und 4/4-Takt

Four steps to success

1. **Look at the top number of the key signature (2, 3 or 4)**. It shows the number of beats in a bar. Tap (clap, sing or play on one note) the rhythm, feeling the pulse throughout. Count at least one bar of the time signature in your head to set up the pulse before you tap or play.

2. **Look for patterns**. While tapping the rhythm, look at the melodic shape and notice movement by step, skips, repeated notes and sequences (a short repeated melodic phrase which usually rises or falls by step).

3. **Spot the 1st fingers** and make sure that you know the name of the new note.

4. **Keep going**. Remember, a wrong note or rhythm can be corrected the next time you play it. If you stop, you have doubled the mistake!

Quatre étapes vers la réussite

1. **Observez le chiffre supérieur de l'indication de mesure (2, 3 ou 4)**. Il indique le nombre de pulsations contenues par mesure. Frappez (dans les mains, chantez ou jouez sur une seule note) le rythme tout en maintenant une pulsation intérieure constante. Comptez mentalement au moins une mesure pour installer la pulsation avant de frappez ou de jouer chaque pièce.

2. **Repérez les motifs**. Tout en frappant le rythme, observez les contours de la mélodie et relevez les mouvements par degrés, les sauts d'intervalles, les notes répétées ou les séquences.

3. **Repérez la première position des doigts** et assurez-vous de connaître le nom de chaque nouvelle note.

4. **Ne vous arrêtez pas**. N'oubliez pas que vous pourrez corriger une fausse note ou un rythme inexact la prochaine fois que vous jouerez. En vous interrompant, vous doublez la faute !

Vier Schritte zum Erfolg

1. **Schaue dir die obere Zahl der Taktangabe an (2, 3 oder 4)**. Diese zeigt die Anzahl der Schläge in einem Takt an. Schlage (klatsche, singe oder spiele auf einer Note) den Rhythmus, wobei du immer das Metrum spürst. Zähle mindestens einen Takt lang die Taktangabe im Kopf, um das Metrum zu verinnerlichen, bevor du klopfst oder spielst.

2. **Achte auf Muster**. Schaue dir die melodische Form an, während du den Rhythmus schlägst und achte auf Bewegungen in Schritten oder Sprüngen, sich wiederholende Noten und Sequenzen (eine kurze, sich wiederholende melodische Phrase, die oft schrittweise ansteigt oder abfällt).

3. **Suche die Noten, bei denen du den 1. Finger brauchst** und versichere dich, dass du die Namen der neuen Note weißt.

4. **Spiele immer weiter**. Denke daran: eine falsche Note oder ein falscher Rhythmus kann beim nächsten Mal korrigiert werden. Wenn du aber aufhörst zu spielen, verdoppelst du den Fehler!

Section 2 – Open strings in 2-, 3- and 4-time
Section 2 – Cordes à vide dans des mesures à 2, 3 et 4 temps
Teil 2 – Leere Saiten im 2/4-, 3/4- und 4/4-Takt

16

Introducing the 1st finger. Introduction du 1er doigt. Einführung des 1. Fingers.

18

Both parts may be played by the
pupil or pupils.

Les deux parties peuvent être jouées
par l'élève ou par deux élèves.

Beide Stimmen können von
Schüler und Lehrer oder von
zwei Schülern gespielt werden.

48.

49.

50.

51.

52.

53.

This piece begins on the third beat of the bar in 3-time.
Count 1 2 3 1 2 before you begin.

Cette pièce débute sur le 3e temps d'une mesure à 3 temps.
Comptez 1, 2, 3, 1, 2, avant de commencer.

Dieses Stück beginnt auf dem dritten Schlag in einem 3/4-Takt.
Zähle 1 2 3 1 2 vor, bevor du anfängst.

54.

Andante

55.

56.

57.

Moderato

Section 3 – Adding the 2nd finger
Section 3 – Introduction du 2ème doigt
Teil 3 – Einführung des 2. Fingers

Five steps to success

1. **Look at the top number of the time signature.** Tap (clap, sing or play on one note) the rhythm, feeling the pulse throughout. Count at least one bar of the time signature in your head to set up the pulse before you tap or play.

2. **Look between the treble clef and the time signature for any sharps and flats.** Make sure you know which notes these apply to and notice where they occur in the melody.

3. **Look for patterns** in both the rhythms and in the melodic shape, and notice movement by step, skips, repeated notes and sequences.

4. **Identify the new fingers on the stave** and say the name of each note.

5. **Keep going!**

Terms and performance directions used in the accompanied pieces: (You may note all directions and translations on the glossary page at the back of the book).

Andante	at a walking pace
Dolce	sweetly
Moderato	at a moderate tempo
Rit. (ritenuto)	gradually getting slower

Cinq étapes vers la réussite

1. **Observez le chiffre supérieur de l'indication de mesure.** Frappez (dans les mains, chantez ou jouez sur un seule note) le rythme tout en maintenant une pulsation intérieure constante. Comptez mentalement au moins une mesure pour installer la pulsation avant de frapper ou de jouer chaque pièce.

2. **Vérifiez les dièses ou les bémols placés entre la clef de *sol* et les chiffres indicateurs de mesure.** Assurez-vous des notes altérées et repérez-les dans la mélodie.

3. **Repérez les motifs** rythmiques et mélodiques et relevez les déplacements par degrés, les sauts d'intervalles, les notes répétées et les séquences.

4. **Repérez les nouvelles positions des doigts et des notes sur la portée** et dites le nom de chaque note.

5. **Ne vous arrêtez pas !**

Indications d'exécution utilisées dans les pièces accompagnées : (Vous pourrez noter toutes les indications et leur traduction sur la page de glossaire en fin de volume).

Andante	allant
Dolce	doux
Moderato	modéré
Rit. (ritenuto)	en retenant progressivement le tempo

Fünf Schritte zum Erfolg

1. **Schaue dir die obere Zahl der Taktangabe an.** Schlage (klatsche, singe oder spiele auf einer Note) den Rhythmus, wobei du immer das Metrum spürst. Zähle mindestens einen Takt lang die Taktangabe im Kopf, um das Metrum zu verinnerlichen, bevor du klopfst oder spielst.

2. **Achte auf Kreuz- und B-Vorzeichen zwischen dem Notenschlüssel und der Taktangabe.** Überzeuge dich davon, dass du weißt, auf welche Noten sich diese beziehen und finde heraus, wo sie in der Melodie auftauchen.

3. **Achte auf Muster:** zum einen bei den Rhythmen und der melodischen Form, zum anderen bei Bewegungen in Schritten oder Sprüngen, sich wiederholende Noten und Sequenzen.

4. **Finde den neu hinzukommenden Finger im Notensystem** und sage den Namen jeder Note.

5. **Spiele immer weiter!**

Begriffe und Vortragsangaben, die bei den begleiteten Stücken verwendet werden: (Du kannst dir alle Angaben und ihre Übersetzungen in der Anhangseite hinten im Buch notieren).

Andante	gehend
Dolce	süß
Moderato	gemäßigt
Rit. (ritenuto)	allmählich langsamer werdend

Section 3 – Adding the 2nd finger
Section 3 – Introduction du 2ème doigt
Teil 3 – Einführung des 2. Fingers

In this section, the 2nd finger will be one tone above the 1st finger.

Dans cette section le 2ème doigt jouera un ton au-dessus du premier.

In diesem Abschnitt wird der 2. Finger immer einen Ganzton über den 1. Finger gesetzt.

The key signature of G major.

Armure de la tonalité de *sol* majeur.

Die Tonart G-Dur.

58.

The key signature of D major.

Armure de la tonalité de *ré* majeur.

Die Tonart D-Dur.

59.

The key signature of A major.

Armure de la tonalité de *la* majeur.

Die Tonart A-Dur.

60.

A major.

la majeur.

A-Dur.

61.

A major.

la majeur.

A-Dur.

62.

D major.

ré majeur.

D-Dur.

63.

24

A major.   *la* majeur.   **A-Dur.**

69.

G major.   *sol* majeur.   **G-Dur.**

70.

71.

72.

73.

74.

75.

76.

77.

Andante

78.

79.

Section 4 – Using the 3rd finger in major keys
Section 4 – Introduction du 3ème doigt dans les tonalités majeures
Teil 4 – Einführung des 3. Fingers in Dur-Tonarten

Five steps to success

1. **Look at the top number of the time signature**. Tap (clap, sing or play on one note) the rhythm, feeling the pulse throughout. Count at least one bar of the time signature in your head to set up the pulse before you tap or play.

2. **Look between the treble clef and the time signature to see how many sharps are in the key signature**. Make sure you know which notes these apply to and notice where they occur in the melody.

3. **Look for patterns**. While tapping the rhythms, look at the melodic shape and notice movement by step, skips, repeated notes and sequences.

4. **Identify the new fingers on the stave** and say the name of each note.

5. **Keep going!**

Terms and performance directions used in the duets and accompanied pieces:

Adagio	slowly
Allegretto	moderately fast
Cantabile	in a singing style
Con moto	with vigour
Grazioso	gracefully
Maestoso	majestically
Moderato	at a moderate tempo
Vivace	lively
Waltz	a dance in three-time

Cinq étapes vers la réussite

1. **Observez le chiffre supérieur de l'indication de mesure**. Frappez (dans les mains, chantez ou jouez sur un seule note) le rythme tout en maintenant une pulsation intérieure constante. Comptez mentalement au moins une mesure pour installer la pulsation avant de frapper ou de jouer chaque pièce.

2. **Vérifiez les dièses ou les bémols placés entre la clef de *sol* et les chiffres indicateurs de mesure**. Assurez-vous des notes altérées et repérez-les dans la mélodie.

3. **Repérez les motifs**. Tout en frappant le rythme, observez les contours de la mélodie et relevez les déplacements par degrés, les sauts d'intervalles, les notes répétées et les séquences.

4. **Repérez les nouvelles positions des doigts et des notes sur la portée** et dites le nom de chaque note.

5. **Ne vous arrêtez pas !**

Indications d'exécution utilisées dans les pièces accompagnées :

Adagio	lent
Allegretto	assez vite
Cantabile	chantant
Con moto	avec force
Grazioso	gracieux
Maestoso	majestueux
Moderato	modéré
Vivace	vif
Valse	danse à trois temps

Fünf Schritte zum Erfolg

1. **Schaue dir die obere Zahl der Taktangabe an**. Schlage (klatsche, singe oder spiele auf einer Note) den Rhythmus, wobei du immer das Metrum spürst. Zähle mindestens einen Takt lang die Taktangabe im Kopf, um das Metrum zu verinnerlichen, bevor du klopfst oder spielst.

2. **Schaue zwischen den Notenschlüssel und die Taktangabe, um zu sehen, wie viele Kreuzvorzeichen die Tonart hat**. Überzeuge dich davon, dass du weißt, auf welche Noten sich diese beziehen und finde heraus, wo in der Melodie sie auftauchen.

3. **Achte auf Muster**. Schaue dir die melodische Form an, während du den Rhythmus schlägst und achte auf Bewegungen in Schritten oder Sprüngen, sich wiederholende Noten und Sequenzen.

4. **Finde den neu hinzukommenden Finger im Notensystem** und sage den Namen jeder Note.

5. **Spiele immer weiter!**

Begriffe und Vortragsangaben, die in den Duetten und begleiteten Stücken verwendet werden:

Adagio	langsam
Allegretto	gemäßigt schnell
Cantabile	gesanglich
Con moto	mit Energie
Grazioso	anmutig
Maestoso	majestätisch
Moderato	gemäßigt
Vivace	lebhaft
Waltz	ein Tanz im 3/4-Takt

Section 4 – Using the 3rd finger in major keys
Section 4 – Introduction du 3ème doigt dans les tonalités majeures
Teil 4 – Einführung des 3. Fingers in Dur-Tonarten

In this section, the 3rd finger always goes one semitone above the 2nd finger.

Clap and sing the following exercises before you play.

Dans cette section, le 3ème doigt joue toujours un demi-ton au-dessus du 2ème doigt.

Frappez dans les mains et chantez les exercices suivant avant de les jouer.

In diesem Abschnitt wird der 3. Finger immer einen Halbton über den 2. Finger gesetzt.

Klatsche und singe die folgenden Übungen bevor du anfängst.

G major.　　　　　　　　　*sol* majeur.　　　　　　　　　G-Dur.

80.

D major.　　　　　　　　　*ré* majeur.　　　　　　　　　D-Dur.

81.

A major.　　　　　　　　　*la* majeur.　　　　　　　　　A-Dur.

82.

E major.　　　　　　　　　*mi* majeur.　　　　　　　　　E-Dur.

83.

Introducing quavers (eighth notes).

This piece begins on the third beat of the bar in 3-time.
Count 1 2 3 1 2 before you begin.

Introduction des croches.

Cette pièce débute sur le 3e temps d'une mesure à 3 temps.
Comptez 1, 2, 3, 1, 2, avant de commencer.

Einführung von Achteln.

Dieses Stück beginnt auf dem dritten Schlag in einem 3/4-Takt.
Zähle 1 2 3 1 2 vor, bevor du anfängst.

84.

32

This piece begins on the third beat
of the bar in 3-time.
Count 1 2 3 1 2 before you begin.

Cette pièce débute sur le 3e temps
d'une mesure à 3 temps.
Comptez 1, 2, 3, 1, 2, avant de
commencer.

Dieses Stück beginnt auf dem
dritten Schlag in einem 3/4-Takt.
Zähle 1 2 3 1 2 vor, bevor du
anfängst.

85.

86.

87.

88.

This piece begins on the third beat
of the bar in 3-time.
Count 1 2 3 1 2 before you begin.

Cette pièce débute sur le 3e temps
d'une mesure à 3 temps.
Comptez 1, 2, 3, 1, 2, avant de
commencer.

Dieses Stück beginnt auf dem
dritten Schlag in einem 3/4-Takt.
Zähle 1 2 3 1 2 vor, bevor du
anfängst.

89.

This piece begins on the third beat of the bar in 3-time.
Count 1 2 3 1 2 before you begin.

Cette pièce débute sur le 3e temps d'une mesure à 3 temps.
Comptez 1, 2, 3, 1, 2, avant de commencer.

Dieses Stück beginnt auf dem dritten Schlag in einem 3/4-Takt.
Zähle 1 2 3 1 2 vor, bevor du anfängst.

90.

91.

92.

Maestoso

93.

Grazioso

94.

95.

96.

This piece begins on the fourth beat of the bar in 4-time. Count 1 2 3 before you begin.

Cette pièce débute sur le 4e temps d'une mesure à 4 temps. Comptez 1, 2, 3, avant de commencer.

Dieses Stück beginnt auf dem vierten Schlag in einem 4/4-Takt. Zähle 1 2 3 vor, bevor du anfängst.

97.

Adagio

Slow waltz.   Valse lente.   Langsamer Walzer.

98.

99.

Section 5 – New keys: C major, F major and B♭ major

Section 5 – Nouvelles tonalités : *do* majeur, *fa* majeur, *si*♭ majeur

Teil 5 – Neue Tonarten: C-Dur, F-Dur und B-Dur

Five steps to success

1. **Look at the top number of the time signature**. Tap (clap, sing or play on one note) the rhythm, feeling the pulse throughout. Count at least one bar of the time signature in your head to set up the pulse before you tap or play.

2. **Look between the treble clef and the time signature**. You will see either one or two flats or none at all in the key signature. Learn these new keys and make sure you know which notes the new flats apply to and where they occur in the melody.

3. **Look for patterns**. While tapping the rhythms, look at the melodic shape and notice movement by step, skips, repeated notes and sequences.

4. **Be aware of the new notes and keys**.

5. **Keep going!**

Terms and performance directions used in the duets and accompanied pieces:

Andante	at a walking pace
Allegro ma non troppo	
	fast, but not too fast
Con moto	with vigour
Dolce	sweetly
Grazioso	gracefully
Maestoso	majestically
Moderato	at a moderate tempo
Poco	a little
Poco adagio	a little slowly
Risoluto	resolutely

Cinq étapes vers la réussite

1. **Observez le chiffre supérieur de l'indication de mesure**. Frappez (dans les mains, chantez ou jouez sur un seule note) le rythme tout en maintenant une pulsation intérieure constante. Comptez mentalement au moins une mesure pour installer la pulsation avant de frapper ou de jouer chaque pièce.

2. **Vérifiez l'armure placée entre la clef de *sol* et les chiffres indicateurs de mesure**. Vous constaterez la présence d'un bémol, de deux bémols ou d'aucun bémol à l'armure de la clef. Apprenez ces nouvelles tonalités et assurez-vous de connaître les notes bémolisées et de les repérer dans la mélodie.

3. **Repérez les motifs**. Tout en frappant les rythmes, observez les contours de la mélodie et relevez les déplacements par degrés, les sauts d'intervalles, les notes répétées et les séquences.

4. **Repérez les nouvelles notes et tonalités**.

5. **Ne vous arrêtez pas !**

Termes et indications d'exécution utilisés dans les duos et les pièces accompagnées :

Andante	allant
Allegro ma non troppo	
	rapide mais pas trop
Con moto	avec force
Dolce	doux
Grazioso	gracieux
Maestoso	majestueux
Moderato	modéré
Poco	un peu
Poco adagio	un peu lent
Risoluto	résolu

Fünf Schritte zum Erfolg

1. **Schau dir die obere Zahl der Taktangabe an**. Schlage (klatsche, singe oder spiele auf einer Note) den Rhythmus, wobei du immer das Metrum spürst. Zähle mindestens einen Takt lang die Taktangabe im Kopf, um das Metrum zu verinnerlichen, bevor du klopfst oder spielst.

2. **Schaue zwischen Notenschlüssel und Taktangabe**. Du wirst entweder ein, zwei oder gar kein B-Vorzeichen finden. Lerne sie und überzeuge dich davon, dass du weißt, auf welche Noten sich diese neuen B-Vorzeichen beziehen und wo sie in der Melodie auftauchen.

3. **Achte auf Muster**. Schaue dir die melodische Form an, während du den Rhythmus schlägst und achte auf Bewegungen in Schritten oder Sprüngen, sich wiederholende Noten und Sequenzen.

4. **Sei dir der neuen Noten und Vorzeichen bewusst**.

5. **Spiele immer weiter!**

Begriffe und Vortragsangaben, die in den Duetten und begleiteten Stücken verwendet werden:

Andante	gehend
Allegro ma non troppo	
	schnell, aber nicht zu schnell
Con moto	mit Bewegung
Dolce	süß
Grazioso	anmutig
Maestoso	majestätisch
Moderato	gemäßigt
Poco	ein wenig
Poco adagio	ein wenig langsam
Risoluto	entschieden

Section 5 – New keys: C major, F major and B♭ major
Section 5 – Nouvelles tonalités : *do* majeur, *fa* majeur, *si*♭ majeur
Teil 5 – Neue Tonarten: C-Dur, F-Dur und B-Dur

107.

F major.   *fa* majeur.   F-Dur.

108.

109.

Mixed keys.   Tonalités diverses.   Verschiedene Tonarten.

110.

111.

112.

113.

114.

40

115.

116.

117.

118.

This piece begins on the fourth beat of the bar in 4-time.
Count 1 2 3 before you begin.

Cette pièce débute sur le 4e temps d'une mesure à 4 temps.
Comptez 1, 2, 3, avant de commencer.

Dieses Stück beginnt auf dem vierten Schlag in einem 4/4-Takt.
Zähle 1 2 3 vor, bevor du anfängst.

119.

This piece begins on the third beat of the bar in 3-time.
Count 1 2 3 1 2 before you begin.

Cette pièce débute sur le 3e temps d'une mesure à 3 temps.
Comptez 1, 2, 3, 1, 2, avant de commencer.

Dieses Stück beginnt auf dem dritten Schlag in einem 3/4-Takt.
Zähle 1 2 3 1 2 vor, bevor du anfängst.

120.

121.

Poco adagio

122.

Con moto

123.

Maestoso

This piece begins on the third beat of the bar in 3-time.
Count 1 2 3 1 2 before you begin.

Cette pièce débute sur le 3e temps d'une mesure à 3 temps.
Comptez 1, 2, 3, 1, 2, avant de commencer.

Dieses Stück beginnt auf dem dritten Schlag in einem 3/4-Takt.
Zähle 1 2 3 1 2 vor, bevor du anfängst.

124.

Grazioso

125.

Allegro ma non troppo

42

This piece begins on the third beat of the bar in 3-time.
Count 1 2 3 1 2 before you begin.

Cette pièce débute sur le 3e temps d'une mesure à 3 temps.
Comptez 1, 2, 3, 1, 2, avant de commencer.

Dieses Stück beginnt auf dem dritten Schlag in einem 3/4-Takt.
Zähle 1 2 3 1 2 vor, bevor du anfängst.

126.

Andante

127.

Moderato

This piece begins on the third beat of the bar in 3-time.
Count 1 2 3 1 2 before you begin.

Cette pièce débute sur le 3e temps d'une mesure à 3 temps.
Comptez 1, 2, 3, 1, 2, avant de commencer.

Dieses Stück beginnt auf dem dritten Schlag in einem 3/4-Takt.
Zähle 1 2 3 1 2 vor, bevor du anfängst.

128.

Risoluto

129.

Quick waltz.   Valse rapide.   Schneller Walzer.

130.

Section 6 – New rhythms and slurs
Section 6 – Nouveaux rythmes et liaisons de phrasé
Teil 6 – Neue Rhythmen und Bindungen

Six steps to success

1. **Look at the top number of the time signature.** Tap (clap, sing or play on one note) the rhythm, feeling the pulse throughout. Count at least one bar in your head to set up the pulse before you tap or play.

2. **Look between the treble clef and the time signature for any sharps or flats.** This is known as the key signature. Make sure you know which notes these apply to and where they occur in the melody.

3. **Look for patterns.** While tapping the rhythm, look at the melodic shape and notice movement by step, skips, repeated notes and sequences.

4. **Look out for accidentals.** You will need to watch for additional sharps, flats or naturals, particularly when playing in minor keys.

5. **Notice the articulation and dynamics.** Observe the dynamic shape and notice if the changes are sudden or gradual.

6. **Keep going!**

Six étapes vers la réussite

1. **Observez l'indication de mesure.** Frappez (dans les mains, chantez ou jouez sur une seule note) le rythme tout en maintenant une pulsation intérieure constante. Comptez mentalement au moins une mesure pour installer la pulsation avant de frapper le rythme ou de jouer la pièce.

2. **Vérifiez les dièses et les bémols placés entre la clef de *sol* et l'indication de mesure.** Ils constituent l'armure de la tonalité. Assurez vous des notes altérées et repérez-les dans la mélodie.

3. **Repérez les motifs.** Tout en frappant le rythme, observez les contours de la mélodie et relevez les mouvements par degré, les sauts d'intervalles, les notes répétées et les séquences.

4. **Recherchez les altérations accidentelles.** Soyez attentif aux dièses, bémols ou bécarres ajoutés, surtout dans les tonalités mineures.

5. **Observez le phrasé et les nuances.** Examinez les formes dynamiques et notez leurs changements subits ou progressifs.

6. **Ne vous arrêtez pas !**

Sechs Schritte zum Erfolg

1. **Schaue dir die obere Zahl der Taktangabe an.** Schlage (klatsche, singe oder spiele auf einer Note) den Rhythmus, wobei du immer das Metrum spürst. Zähle mindestens einen Takt lang die Taktangabe im Kopf, um das Metrum zu verinnerlichen, bevor du klopfst oder spielst.

2. **Schaue zwischen Notenschlüssel und Taktangabe nach Kreuz- oder B-Vorzeichen.** Diese ergeben die Tonart. Vergewissere dich, dass du weißt, auf welche Noten sie sich beziehen und wo sie in der Melodie auftauchen.

3. **Achte auf Muster.** Schaue dir die melodische Form an, während du den Rhythmus schlägst und achte auf Bewegungen in Schritten oder Sprüngen, sich wiederholende Noten und Sequenzen.

4. **Suche nach Vorzeichen im Stück.** Du musst nach zusätzlichen Kreuzen, Bs oder Auflösungszeichen Ausschau halten, besonders bei den Stücken, die in einer Molltonart stehen.

5. **Beachte Artikulation und Dynamik.** Schaue die Dynamikzeichen genau an und erkenne, ob die Veränderungen plötzlich oder allmählich sind.

6. **Spiele immer weiter!**

Terms and performance directions used in this section:

Adagio	slowly
Alla marcia	in the style of a march
Allegretto	moderately fast
Andante	at walking pace
Andantino	a little faster than Andante
Con grazia	with grace
Con moto	with vigour
Dolce	sweetly
Gavotte	a lively dance beginning on the 3rd beat
Grazioso	gracefully
Maestoso	majestically
Mesto	sadly
Moderato	at a moderate tempo
Poco adagio	a little slowly
Poco allegro	a little fast
Poco lento	a little slowly
Risoluto	resolutely
Ritmico	rhythmically
Tranquillo	tranquil
Vivace	lively
Vivo	lively

Termes et indications d'exécutions utilisés dans cette section :

Adagio	lent
Alla marcia	en style de marche
Allegretto	assez rapide
Andante	allant
Andantino	un peu plus vite qu'Andante
Con grazia	avec grâce
Con moto	avec force
Dolce	doux
Gavotte	danse vive commençant sur le 3ème temps
Grazioso	gracieux
Maestoso	majestueux
Mesto	triste
Moderato	modéré
Poco adagio	un peu lent
Poco allegro	un peu rapide
Poco lento	un peu lent
Risoluto	résolu
Ritmico	rythmique
Tranquillo	tranquille
Vivace	vif
Vivo	vif

Begriffe und Vortragsangaben, die in diesem Teil verwendet werden:

Adagio	langsam
Alla marcia	marschmäßig
Allegretto	gemäßigt schnell
Andante	gehend
Andantino	ein bisschen schneller als Andante
Con grazia	mit Anmut
Con moto	mit Energie
Dolce	süß
Gavotte	ein lebhafter Tanz, der auf dem dritten Schlag beginnt
Grazioso	anmutig
Maestoso	majestätisch
Mesto	traurig
Moderato	gemäßigt
Poco adagio	ein wenig langsam
Poco allegro	ein wenig schnell
Poco lento	ein wenig langsam
Risoluto	entschieden
Ritmico	rhythmisch
Tranquillo	ruhig
Vivace	lebhaft
Vivo	lebhaft

Section 6 – New rhythms and slurs
Section 6 – Nouveaux rythmes et liaisons de phrasé
Teil 6 – Neue Rhythmen und Bindungen

131.

132.

This piece begins on the second beat of the bar in 2-time. Count 1 2 1 before you begin.	Cette pièce débute sur le 2e temps d'une mesure à 2 temps. Comptez 1, 2, 1, avant de commencer.	Dieses Stück beginnt auf dem zweiten Schlag in einem 2/4-Takt. Zähle 1 2 1 vor, bevor du anfängst.

133.

This piece begins on the second beat of the bar in 2-time. Count 1 2 1 before you begin.	Cette pièce débute sur le 2e temps d'une mesure à 2 temps. Comptez 1, 2, 1, avant de commencer.	Dieses Stück beginnt auf dem zweiten Schlag in einem 2/4-Takt. Zähle 1 2 1 vor, bevor du anfängst.

134.

135.

136.

48

137.

Dolce

mp

138.

Moderato

mf

139.

Vivace

f

140.

Andantino

mp

141.

Risoluto

mf

142.

Maestoso

f

143.

Ritmico

mf

144.

Moderato

mf

145.

Andantino

Minor keys.   Tonalités mineures.   Moll-Tonarten.

G minor.   *sol* mineur.   g-Moll.

146.

Poco adagio

147.

Moderato

D minor.   *ré* mineur.   d-Moll.

148.

Allegretto

149.

Andante

A minor.   *la* mineur.   a-Moll.

150.

Grazioso

151.

Ritmico

152.

Con grazia

This piece begins on the third beat of the bar in 3-time.
Count 1 2 3 1 2 before you begin.

Cette pièce débute sur le 3e temps d'une mesure à 3 temps.
Comptez 1, 2, 3, 1, 2, avant de commencer.

Dieses Stück beginnt auf dem dritten Schlag in einem 3/4-Takt.
Zähle 1 2 3 1 2 vor, bevor du anfängst.

153.

Con moto

This piece begins on the fourth beat of the bar in 4-time.
Count 1 2 3 before you begin.

Cette pièce débute sur le 4e temps d'une mesure à 4 temps.
Comptez 1, 2, 3, avant de commencer.

Dieses Stück beginnt auf dem vierten Schlag in einem 4/4-Takt.
Zähle 1 2 3 vor, bevor du anfängst.

154.

Alla marcia

This piece begins on the third beat of the bar in 3-time.
Count 1 2 3 1 2 before you begin.

Cette pièce débute sur le 3e temps d'une mesure à 3 temps.
Comptez 1, 2, 3, 1, 2, avant de commencer.

Dieses Stück beginnt auf dem dritten Schlag in einem 3/4-Takt.
Zähle 1 2 3 1 2 vor, bevor du anfängst.

155.

156.

157.

158.

Tranquillo

159.

Adagio

This piece begins on the third beat of the bar in 3-time.
Count 1 2 3 1 2 before you begin.

Cette pièce débute sur le 3e temps d'une mesure à 3 temps.
Comptez 1, 2, 3, 1, 2, avant de commencer.

Dieses Stück beginnt auf dem dritten Schlag in einem 3/4-Takt.
Zähle 1 2 3 1 2 vor, bevor du anfängst.

160.

Andante

This piece begins on the third beat of the bar in 4-time.
Count 1 2 3 4 1 2 before you begin.

Cette pièce débute sur le 3e temps d'une mesure à 4 temps.
Comptez 1, 2, 3, 4, 1, 2, avant de commencer.

Dieses Stück beginnt auf dem dritten Schlag in einem 4/4-Takt.
Zähle 1 2 3 4 1 2 vor, bevor du anfängst.

161.

Gavotte

This piece begins on the fourth
beat of the bar in 4-time.
Count 1 2 3 before you begin.

Cette pièce débute sur le 4e temps
d'une mesure à 4 temps.
Comptez 1, 2, 3, avant de commencer.

Dieses Stück beginnt auf dem
vierten Schlag in einem 4/4-Takt.
Zähle 1 2 3 vor, bevor du anfängst.

162.

This piece begins on the fourth
beat of the bar in 4-time.
Count 1 2 3 before you begin.

Cette pièce débute sur le 4e temps
d'une mesure à 4 temps.
Comptez 1, 2, 3, avant de commencer.

Dieses Stück beginnt auf dem
vierten Schlag in einem 4/4-Takt.
Zähle 1 2 3 vor, bevor du anfängst.

163.

164.

This piece begins on the fourth beat of the bar in 4-time. Count 1 2 3 before you begin.

Cette pièce débute sur le 4e temps d'une mesure à 4 temps. Comptez 1, 2, 3, avant de commencer.

Dieses Stück beginnt auf dem vierten Schlag in einem 4/4-Takt. Zähle 1 2 3 vor, bevor du anfängst.

165.

Section 7 – Counting quaver beats in 3/8 time
Section 7 – Battue des croches dans la mesure à 3/8
Teil 7 – Der 3/8-Takt

Six steps to success

1. **Look at the top number of the time signature.** Tap (clap, sing or play on one note) the rhythm, feeling the pulse throughout. Count at least one bar in your head to set up the tempo before you tap or play.

2. **Look between the treble clef and the time signature for any sharps or flats.** This is the key signature. Make sure you know which notes these apply to and where they occur in the melody.

3. **Look for patterns.** While tapping the rhythm, look at the melodic shape and notice movement by step, skips, repeated notes and sequences.

4. **Look out for accidentals.** You will need to watch for additional sharps, flats or naturals, particularly when playing in minor keys.

5. **Notice the articulation and dynamics.** Observe the dynamic shape and notice if the changes are sudden or gradual.

6. **Keep going!**

Terms and performance directions used in the duets and accompanied pieces:
Allegro vivace   fast and lively
Andante sostenuto
     at a walking pace and sustained
Mesto   sadly
Mesto sostenuto
     sadly and sustained
Poco lento   a little slowly
Risoluto   resolutely
Sostenuto   sustained
Vivace   lively

Six étapes vers la réussite

1. **Observez l'indication de mesure.** Frappez (dans les mains, chantez ou jouez sur une seule note) le rythme tout en maintenant une pulsation intérieure constante. Comptez mentalement au moins une mesure pour installer la pulsation avant de frapper le rythme ou de jouer la pièce.

2. **Vérifiez les dièses ou les bémols placés entre la clef de *sol* et l'indication de mesure.** Ils constituent l'armure de la tonalité. Assurez vous des notes altérées et repérez-les dans la mélodie.

3. **Repérez les motifs.** Tout en frappant le rythme, observez les contours de la mélodie et relevez les mouvements par degré, les sauts d'intervalles, les notes répétées et les séquences.

4. **Recherchez les altérations accidentelles.** Soyez attentifs aux dièses, bémols ou bécarres ajoutés, en particulier dans les tonalités mineures.

5. **Observez le phrasé et les nuances.** Examinez les formes dynamiques et notez leurs changements subits ou progressifs.

6. **Ne vous arrêtez pas !**

Termes et indications d'exécution utilisés dans les duos et les pièces avec accompagnement :
Allegro vivace   rapide et vif
Andante sostenuto
     allant et soutenu
Mesto   triste
Mesto sostenuto   triste et soutenu
Poco lento   un peu lent
Risoluto   résolu
Sostenuto   soutenu
Vivace   vif

Sechs Schritte zum Erfolg

1. **Schaue dir die obere Zahl der Taktangabe an.** Schlage (klatsche, singe oder spiele auf einer Note) den Rhythmus, wobei du immer das Metrum spürst. Zähle mindestens einen Takt lang die Taktangabe im Kopf, um das Metrum zu verinnerlichen, bevor du klopfst oder spielst.

2. **Schaue zwischen Notenschlüssel und Taktangabe nach Kreuz- oder B-Vorzeichen.** Diese zeigen die Tonart an. Vergewissere dich, dass du weißt, auf welche Noten sie sich beziehen und wo sie in der Melodie auftauchen.

3. **Achte auf Muster.** Schaue dir die melodische Form an, während du den Rhythmus schlägst und achte auf Bewegungen in Schritten oder Sprüngen, sich wiederholende Noten und Sequenzen.

4. **Suche nach Vorzeichen im Stück.** Du musst nach zusätzlichen Kreuzen, Bs oder Auflösungszeichen Ausschau halten, besonders bei den Stücken, die in einer Molltonart stehen.

5. **Beachte Artikulation und Dynamik.** Schaue die Dynamikzeichen genau an und erkenne, ob die Veränderungen plötzlich oder allmählich sind.

6. **Spiele immer weiter!**

Begriffe und Vortragsangaben, die in den Duetten und begleiteten Stücken verwendet werden:
Allegro vivace   schnell und lebhaft
Andante sostenuto
     gehend und zurückhaltend
Mesto   traurig
Mesto sostenuto
     traurig und zurückhaltend
Poco lento   ein wenig langsam
Risoluto   entschieden
Sostenuto   zurückhaltend
Vivace   lebhaft

Section 7 – Counting quaver beats in 3/8 time
Section 7 – Battue des croches dans la mesure à 3/8
Teil 7 – Der 3/8-Takt

Play these at a moderate tempo, counting 1 2 3 throughout.

Jouer ces pièces à une allure modérée et sans cesser de compter 1, 2, 3.

Spiele diese Stücke in einem mäßigen Tempo und zähle 1 2 3 vor, bevor du anfängst.

166.

167.

168.

169.

170.

171.

172.

58

Open string shifts.   Déplacements sur les cordes à vide.   Lagenwechsel auf der leeren Saite.

173.

174.

175.

176.

177.

This piece begins on the fourth
beat of the bar in 4-time.
Count 1 2 3 before you begin.

Cette pièce débute sur le 4e temps
d'une mesure à 4 temps.
Comptez 1, 2, 3, avant de commencer.

Dieses Stück beginnt auf dem
vierten Schlag in einem 4/4-Takt.
Zähle 1 2 3 vor, bevor du anfängst.

178.

This piece begins on the third beat of the bar in 3-time.
Count 1 2 3 1 2 before you begin.

Cette pièce débute sur le 3e temps d'une mesure à 3 temps.
Comptez 1, 2, 3, 1, 2, avant de commencer.

Dieses Stück beginnt auf dem dritten Schlag in einem 3/4-Takt.
Zähle 1 2 3 1 2 vor, bevor du anfängst.

179.

180.

181.

182.

This piece begins on the third beat of the bar in 3-time.
Count 1 2 3 1 2 before you begin.

Cette pièce débute sur le 3e temps d'une mesure à 3 temps.
Comptez 1, 2, 3, 1, 2, avant de commencer.

Dieses Stück beginnt auf dem dritten Schlag in einem 3/4-Takt.
Zähle 1 2 3 1 2 vor, bevor du anfängst.

183.

184.

This piece begins on the third beat of the bar in 3-time.
Count 1 2 3 1 2 before you begin.

Cette pièce débute sur le 3e temps d'une mesure à 3 temps.
Comptez 1, 2, 3, 1, 2, avant de commencer.

Dieses Stück beginnt auf dem dritten Schlag in einem 3/4-Takt.
Zähle 1 2 3 1 2 vor, bevor du anfängst.

185.

186.

187.

188.

Poco lento

189.

Vivace

190.

Sostenuto

This piece begins on the third beat of the bar in 3-time.
Count 1 2 3 1 2 before you begin.

Cette pièce débute sur le 3e temps d'une mesure à 3 temps.
Comptez 1, 2, 3, 1, 2, avant de commencer.

Dieses Stück beginnt auf dem dritten Schlag in einem 3/8-Takt.
Zähle 1 2 3 1 2 vor, bevor du anfängst.

191.

Risoluto

192.

Vivace

193.

Allegro vivace

This piece begins on the third beat of the bar in 3-time.
Count 1 2 3 1 2 before you begin.

Cette pièce débute sur le 3e temps d'une mesure à 3 temps.
Comptez 1, 2, 3, 1, 2, avant de commencer.

Dieses Stück beginnt auf dem dritten Schlag in einem 3/8-Takt.
Zähle 1 2 3 1 2 vor, bevor du anfängst.

194.

195.

This piece begins on the third beat of the bar in 3-time.
Count 1 2 3 1 2 before you begin.

Cette pièce débute sur le 3e temps d'une mesure à 3 temps.
Comptez 1, 2, 3, 1, 2, avant de commencer.

Dieses Stück beginnt auf dem dritten Schlag in einem 3/8-Takt.
Zähle 1 2 3 1 2 vor, bevor du anfängst.

196.

197.

Section 8 – Compound time
Section 8 – Mesures composées
Teil 8 – Zusammengesetzte Taktarten

Six steps to success

1. **Look at the top number of the time signature.** Tap (clap, sing, or play on one note) the rhythm, feeling the pulse throughout. Count at least one bar in your head to set up the tempo before you tap or play.

2. **Look between the treble clef and the time signature for any sharps and flats.** This is the key signature. Make sure you know which notes these apply to and where they occur in the melody.

3. **Look for patterns.** While tapping the rhythm, look at the melodic shape and notice movement by step, skips, repeated notes and sequences.

4. **Look for accidentals.** You will need to watch for additional sharps, flats or naturals, particularly when playing in minor keys.

5. **Notice the articulation and dynamics.** Observe the dynamic shape and notice if the changes are sudden or gradual.

6. **Keep going!**

New terms and performance directions used in this section:
Barcarolle a 'boat song' derived from the Venetian Gondoliers
Energetico energetically
Ritmico rhythmically
Tarantella a lively dance from Taranto in southern Italy, supposedly a cure for the bite of a tarantula!

Six étapes vers la réussite

1. **Observez l'indication de mesure.** Frappez (dans les mains, chantez ou jouez sur une seule note) le rythme tout en maintenant une pulsation intérieure constante. Comptez mentalement au moins une mesure pour installer la pulsation avant de frapper le rythme ou de jouer la pièce.

2. **Vérifiez les dièses ou les bémols placés entre la clef de *sol* et l'indication de mesure.** Ils constituent l'armure de la tonalité. Assurez vous des notes altérées et repérez-les dans la mélodie.

3. **Repérez les motifs.** Tout en frappant le rythme, observez les contours de la mélodie et relevez les mouvements par degré, les sauts d'intervalles, les notes répétées et les séquences.

4. **Recherchez les altérations accidentelles.** Soyez attentifs aux dièses, bémols ou bécarres ajoutés, en particulier dans les tonalités mineures.

5. **Observez le phrasé et les nuances.** Examinez les formes dynamiques et notez leurs changements subits ou progressifs.

6. **Ne vous arrêtez pas !**

Nouveaux termes et indications d'exécution utilisés dans cette section :
Barcarolle chant de gondoliers
Energetico énergique
Ritmico rythmique
Tarantella Tarentelle, danse originaire de Tarente dans le sud de l'Italie, supposée guérir des morsures d'araignées (*tarantula*)

Sechs Schritte zum Erfolg

1. **Schaue dir die obere Zahl der Taktangabe an.** Schlage (klatsche, singe oder spiele auf einer Note) den Rhythmus, wobei du immer das Metrum spürst. Zähle mindestens einen Takt lang die Taktangabe im Kopf, um das Metrum zu verinnerlichen, bevor du klopfst oder spielst.

2. **Schaue zwischen Notenschlüssel und Taktangabe nach Kreuz- oder B-Vorzeichen.** Diese zeigen die Tonart an. Vergewissere dich, dass du weißt, auf welche Noten sie sich beziehen und wo sie in der Melodie auftauchen.

3. **Achte auf Muster.** Schaue dir die melodische Form an, während du den Rhythmus schlägst und achte auf Bewegungen in Schritten oder Sprüngen, sich wiederholende Noten und Sequenzen.

4. **Suche nach Vorzeichen im Stück.** Du musst nach zusätzlichen Kreuzen, Bs oder Auflösungszeichen Ausschau halten, besonders bei den Stücken, die in einer Molltonart stehen.

5. **Beachte Artikulation und Dynamik.** Schaue die Dynamikzeichen genau an und erkenne, ob die Veränderungen plötzlich oder allmählich sind.

6. **Spiele immer weiter!**

Neue Begriffe und Vortragsangaben, die in diesem Teil verwendet werden:
Barcarolle ein 'Bootslied', das von den venetianischen Gondoliere abstammt
Energetico voller Energie
Ritmico rhythmisch
Tarantella ein lebhafter Tanz aus Tarent in Süditalien; angeblich einHeilmittel gegen den Biß der Tarantel!

Key steps to understanding compound rhythms

1. 6/8, 9/8 and 12/8 are known as compound time signatures. Each beat is divided into three equal parts (say the word 'elephant' to a beat), unlike simple time signatures (2/4, 3/4 and 4/4), which divide into two equal parts (say the word 'tiger' to a beat).

2. 6/8 is the most common of these time signatures and means six equal quavers (eighth notes) in a bar. In 6/8 there are two groups of three quavers (eighth notes), so each bar has two beats and will be counted in two.

3. The opening two bars of 'Humpty Dumpty' contain the three most common rhythms found in compound time signatures.

4. In all compound time signatures

♩. = two beats

♪. = one beat

♩ = two thirds of a beat

♪ = one third of a beat

5.
6/8 is two beats in a bar
(two groups of three quavers)

9/8 is three beats in a bar
(three groups of three quavers)

12/8 is four beats in a bar
(four groups of three quavers)

Etapes essentielles à la compréhension des mesures composées

1. 6/8, 9/8 et 12/8 constituent les indications de mesures composées. Chaque temps y est divisé en trois parties égales (prononcez le mot « éléphant » sur chaque temps) à la différence des mesures simples (2/4, 3/4, et 4/4) dont les temps se divisent en deux parties égales (prononcez les mot « canard » sur chaque temps).

2. 6/8 est l'indication de mesure composée la plus fréquente et signifie que chaque mesure contient six croches égales. Chaque mesure à 6/8 contient deux groupes de trois croches. C'est donc une mesure à deux temps.

3. Les deux premières mesures de *Humpty Dumpty* présentent les trois rythmes les plus fréquemment rencontrés dans les mesures composées.

4. Dans toutes les mesures composées

♩. = deux temps

♪. = un temps

♩ = deux tiers de temps

♪ = un tiers de temps

5.
6/8 indique deux temps par mesure
(deux groupes de trois croches)

9/8 indique trois temps par mesure
(trois groupes de trois croches)

12/8 indique quatre temps par mesure
(quatre groupes de trois croches)

Die entscheidenden Schritte, um zusammengesetzte Taktarten zu verstehen

1. 6/8, 9/8 und 12/8-Takt sind als zusammengesetzte Taktarten bekannt. Jeder Schlag ist in drei gleichlange Teile aufgeteilt (sage das Wort ‚Murmeltier' auf einen Schlag) im Gegensatz zu einfachen Taktarten (2/4, 3/4 und 4/4), die in zwei gleichlange Teile aufgeteilt sind (sage das Wort ‚Tiger' auf einen Schlag).

2. Von diesen Taktarten kommt der 6/8-Takt am häufigsten vor. Er besteht aus sechs gleichlangen Achteln in einem Takt. Im 6/8-Takt gibt es zwei Gruppen mit je drei Achtelnoten. Jeder Takt hat also zwei Schläge und wird auf ‚zwei' gezählt.

3. Die Eröffnungstakte des Kinderliedes *Humpty Dumpty* beinhalten die drei häufigsten Rhythmen, die man in zusammengesetzten Taktarten finden kann.

4. In allen zusammengesetzten Taktarten sind

♩. = zwei Schläge

♪. = ein Schlag

♩ = 2/3 eines Schlages

♪ = 1/3 eines Schlages

5.
6/8 hat zwei Schläge in einem Takt (zwei Gruppen mit drei Achteln)

9/8 hat drei Schläge in einem Takt (drei Gruppen mit drei Achteln)

12/8 hat vier Schläge in einem Takt (vier Gruppen mit drei Achteln)

Section 8 – Compound time
Section 8 – Mesures composées
Teil 8 – Zusammengesetzte Taktarten

198.

199.

This piece begins after the second beat in 2-time.
Count 1 (2 3) 2 (2) before you begin.

Cette pièce débute après le 2e temps d'une mesure à 2 temps.
Comptez 1 (2, 3), 2 (2) avant de commencer.

Dieses Stück beginnt auf dem letzten Achtel in einem 6/8-Takt.
Zähle 1 (2 3) 2 (2) vor, bevor du anfängst.

200.

This piece begins on the sixth quaver of the bar in 2-time.
At this tempo count 1 (2 3) 4 (5) before you begin.

Cette pièce débute sur la sixième croche d'une mesure à 2 temps.
Comptez 1 (2, 3), 4 (5) à ce tempo avant de commencer.

Dieses Stück beginnt auf dem letzten Achtel in einem 6/8-Takt.
Zähle auf Grund des langsamen Tempos 1 (2 3) 4 (5) vor, bevor du anfängst.

201.

202.

Moderato

203.

Poco lento

This piece begins after the second beat in 2-time.
Count 1 (2 3) 2 (2) before you begin.

Cette pièce débute après le 2e temps d'une mesure à 2 temps.
Comptez 1 (2, 3), 2 (2) avant de commencer.

Dieses Stück beginnt auf dem letzten Achtel in einem 6/8-Takt.
Zähle 1 (2 3) 2 (2) vor, bevor du anfängst.

204.

Allegretto

205.

Ritmico

206.

Andante

207.

Allegro

This piece begins after the third beat in 3-time.
Count 1 (2 3) 2 (2 3) 3 (2) before you begin.

Cette pièce débute après le 3e temps d'une mesure à 3 temps.
Comptez 1 (2, 3), 2 (2, 3), 3 (2) avant de commencer.

Dieses Stück beginnt auf dem letzten Achtel in einem 9/8-Takt.
Zähle 1 (2 3) 2 (2 3) 3 (2) vor, bevor du anfängst.

208.

209.

This piece begins after the third beat in 3-time.
Count 1 (2 3) 2 (2 3) 3 (2) at an appropriate tempo before you begin.

Cette pièce débute après le 3e temps d'une mesure à 3 temps.
Comptez 1 (2, 3), 2 (2, 3), 3 (2) avant de commencer.

Dieses Stück beginnt auf dem letzten Achtel in einem 9/8-Takt.
Zähle 1 (2 3) 2 (2 3) 3 (2) vor, bevor du anfängst.

210.

This piece begins after the third beat in 3-time.
Count a steady 1 (2 3) 2 (2 3) 3 (2) before you begin.

Cette pièce débute après le 3e temps d'une mesure à 3 temps.
Comptez 1 (2, 3), 2 (2, 3), 3 (2) avant de commencer.

Dieses Stück beginnt auf dem letzten Achtel in einem 9/8-Takt.
Zähle 1 (2 3) 2 (2 3) 3 (2) vor, bevor du anfängst.

211.

Cantabile

212.

Vivace

213.

Barcarolle

214.

Allegro vivace (Tarantella)

215.

Glossary
Glossaire
Glossar

Note performance directions together with their translations used throughout the book so that you have a complete list. Writing them down will help you to remember them.

Inscrivez ici les indications d'exécution utilisées dans ce volume et leur traduction pour en établir une liste complète. Le fait de les noter vous aidera à les retenir.

Schreibe hier alle Vortragsangaben, die im Buch verwendet werden, zusammen mit ihrer Übersetzung auf, so dass du eine vollständige Liste hast. Das Aufschreiben wird dir dabei helfen, sie dir einzuprägen.

Adagio	Slowly	Lent	Langsam
